NAPPY

metaphysic

special hardcover edition

Gerald L. Coleman

NAPPY

metaphysic

special hardcover edition

Iconiclast Press
Atlanta, Georgia

ISBN 978-108788988-7

Geraldcoleman.com

Cover Image by Houcine Ncib
Cover Design by Gerald L. Coleman
Cover Layout by Errick Nunnally

Previously published poems in this collection are published in "the long road home" – "falling to earth" – and "microphone check".

as always, for affrilachia ...

Contents

Introduction
Special Edition

Acknowledgments

About the Author

Introduction

In 1986 I made my way to the University of Kentucky, ostensibly, to become an architect. I'd taken some drafting classes in high school, drawn some plans, and made some models – and so I had visions of bow ties, pressed shirts, suspenders, bespoke suits, and buildings as art. I was going to make my mark on the skylines of big cities and on hills overlooking small ones.

In order to get there, I had to make my way through my pre-requisites. In choosing an elective, I decided, on a whim, to take philosophy 101. On the first day of class, Dr. Holbrook entered, wrote his name on the board, turned and asked, "What are you sitting on?"

Of course, someone raised their hand and said, "A chair."

Dr. Holbrook responded, "Are you sure?"

He spent the next 50 minutes utterly deconstructing our reality and the suppositions upon which that perception of reality was based. I was laid low. It took me 20 minutes to gather myself and find the wherewithal to stand up and leave. While some of my fellow classmates ran to the registrar to drop the class, I quietly made my way to my advisor to change my major. I let go of the idea of becoming an architect and instead became a Philosophy and English double major. I know, crazy, right?

All the while, I was writing poetry. It was terrible poetry, but poetry nonetheless. I had only shown it to a couple of the young women I had gone to high school with. It wasn't until I was immersing myself in the life of an undergrad – coffee, cheap food, late hours, and hanging out in the corner of Wildcat grill that I began to wonder why I was alone in it? I must be. Surely, there aren't any other black men writing contemporary poetry.

Then the University was put upon to create a space for African American students and the Martin Luther King Jr. Cultural Center was born. It quickly became the place for black students to call home. And it was there that my real journey in writing began. I met Frank X Walker and discovered a kindred spirit. And we were both relieved to find another brother writing poetry. That meeting would eventually culminate in the creation of the Affrilachian Poets. I went on to study with George Ella Lyon and Nikky Finney. I got to perform with Amiri Baraka (rest in strength) – who told me later that I was talented, and I haven't doubted that since he blessed me with those words. I met Nikki Giovanni (she still has my Waterman pen). And I read in front of Nancy Wilson in Louisville. Ms. Wilson reached out and grabbed my arm on my way back to my seat and confiscated the poems I read, gave me her address, and asked me to send her more. She was personified grace (rest in strength).

But, above all, I participated in the creation of a community of writers and poets – the aforementioned Affrilachian Poets – from which I drew strength and inspiration. Those were halcyon days of going hungry, finding our poetic voices and styles, and claiming the name Poet for ourselves. I have been writing ever since.

This collection is a testament to the last three decades of that ongoing pursuit. The poem that opens this collection, *i, alfred*, was entitled by Nikky Finney after a discussion about names and claiming one's whole self. It was the first poem where I really found my particular voice and style. You can see that style in every poem that follows it. I have written about my childhood, my family, and being a poet –

about love, sex, bourbon, my culture, and all the ways in which being a black man in the country of my birth affects me. I hope this collection moves you. I hope the words you find here matter to you. And I thank you for taking the time to read them. To my teachers, George Ella and Nikky, I say thank you for helping me find my voice. Thank you for your words and your guidance. It is never forgotten. To my mother and brother, I say thank you for your love and your support. And to my writing community – the Affrilachian Poets – I say, pepper, fam, pepper.

Gerald L. Coleman
April 2019
Atlanta, Georgia

Special Edition

These past few weeks have seen drastic turmoil in the *US*. Once again police have murdered black folks. In Minneapolis it was George Floyd and in Louisville it was Breonna Taylor.

One of the ways I deal in these moments is to write. It's not conducive for me to work on my science fiction & fantasy novels or short stories, so I turn to poetry. It's in poetry that I find the framework to express my rage, sorrow, and hope. It's also where I work through how to move forward.

This week I wrote four new poems about how these latest incidents made me feel. I have taken them, and a few other poems not found in the original paperback, and added them here in this special hardcover edition. Rather than go on at length about what it all means, I'll let the poetry speak for itself. As always, Black Lives Matter.

Gerald L. Coleman
June 2, 2020
Atlanta, Georgia

NAPPY

metaphysic

special hardcover edition

i, alfred

(for elwood spaulding, my grandfather)

10:33 am and first
second son was i
born, snuggled warm
in a jamaican
lagoon blue blanket
and put in
a sterilized
fayette county crib
was i

then they came

came to lay
claim to me
those rough
tree-bark handed
hot water cornbread
folk, looking as if
they had just
left the field
the one they
gave up in
flatwoods kin-
tucky
gave it up for
a small pieced
plot of speak-us
hill lexington

they came
came to lay

kin claim to me
they did

little homemade
biscuit and brown
sugar pie annie bell
tree-tall, corn stalk
slim elwood the
spaulding clan's bread
raising, earth tiller
ground guardian
and king, he

came to see
about his baby
girl whom he had
named after his
favorite month
of the year, came
to see his june
and the man child
grand son she had
with God's help
given him

that God whittled
stick of a grand
man came and
peered all dignified
and solemn like
into my blue grass
cradle, standing
there wrinkle-faced
grinning to himself

annie bell ... he said
that boy looks like
alfred hitchcock!
he laughed

no he doesn't
said my mother's
mother, grand and giggling
with a, that's silly, dip
on
the doesn't

my high yella
fresh born face
wide-eyed look
with just enough
fuzz to be called
hair on my head
and my
unmistakably
fat cheeks had
proclaimed to
that grand man
my mother's
father
that i was
alfred

he would not
call me by
the name the
woman who
gave birth to me
had signed to
a clerk's clipboard
no
no
i
i, alfred

alfred i
was called
until the day
he died from
a heart that could

4

not bring itself
to beat one
moment longer
alfred i

alfred to the
kitchen was i
called
called to see
his time and
again prank
his two raw egg
suck plate trick
the one that
to his delight
always sent
me three or was
it four into spasms
as i, the dramatis
personae squirmed
at his feet

i was disgusted
at what that
lovable loved
grand man my
mother's father
had done and
done again and
again, my momma
tellin me later

he only did that
because he knew
it would make you
gag and convulse …

me and he
we
had an

agreement

part of it said
that he would
plate suck eggs
and i would
shiver and gag
another part said
that we
the men that
we were
simply never ate
lest there be
bread
on the table
we rode the
tractor together
staring into each
other's eyes knowing
we were both
closer to God
than the rest
of the world

i was new
just in the front
door, while he
was old, on
his way out
the back
both of us
ancient souls
that knew all
we had was
faith and a
clear conscience

and to this
day though
they, those i

know and others
call me by
my name
i am still
alfred
yeah, alfred

and because
i loved him
love him
that grand man
overalled elder
of my tribe
tractor riding
griot, hoe
and spade warrior

i pay him
wish-he-were-here
homage
giving
hope-he-can-see
respect

i never

ever

sit down
to eat
lest there be
bread
on the table

before it was cool

i was a
nerd before
it was cool

bespectacled
behind a stack
of comics, yeah
i knew that
alcoholic in a
red and gold
alloy-not-iron
suit before
they put his
name in lights
i knew the
blind man
without fear
before they squandered
his devilish
double-d red
reputation in
darkened theaters
with popcorn
littering the floor

back when
clare de lune
was being pumped
into the neighborhood
through grainy
speakers while
star-spangled bomb
pops and orange
pushups were
being pedaled like

it was crack out
of cold trucks
with faded pictures
of frozen happiness
on the side
i was that
shoe unlaced nerd
with luke cage and
iron fist tucked
under my arm

before
it was cool

i was the
quiet little cutie
grown-ass women
fell in love with
my cheeks were
irresistible to
their bejeweled and
lotioned, long
and manicured
face-pinching fingers
i know now
that what i
saw in their
eyes then, was
either a longing
for saddle-shoed
days gone by
or a desperate wish
for a grown up
me

stan lee was
my Shakespeare
before
it was cool

while waiting
for my very
own mutant
powers to manifest
themselves
i was taking apart
all my mother's
electronics
screws, boards,
fuses, tubes all
laid out in a row
i was wired
on dismantled
televisions looking
for the secrets
of the universe
all the while raising
her blood pressure
as she walked in on
her brand new
radio in pieces
giving me that
what-have-i
brought-into-the
world look when
i returned it
reassembled, fully
functional

i was a nerd
before the cool
nonprescription
glasses epidemic
before nostalgia
made chuck taylors
a badge of honor
back when they
were just cheap
before the ironic
t-shirt renaissance

before they made
batman sane

i was a nerd
before
it was cool

and that was cool

back story

luke cage was born
to deflect bullets
as a commentary
on the plight of
black men
we have to be
superheroes
to get through the day

they called him
power man, because
we didn't have any

no cape or cowl
no stylized letter
or animal
on his chest
just bracelets
like handcuffs
around his wrists
and bright colors

see me muthafuka

named after
the very artifice
that
makes us palatable
first named
after a disciple, like a
good church boy
last named after
the place where we

belonged
so everyone else feels safe

back storied
in crime, because
we're all criminal
minded, but redeemable
for the right price
because
we have to be hired
to be heroes

pay me muthafuka

partnered with
a blond white boy
married
to a brunette
because
we need white folks
to co-sign our shit

but somehow, i
still managed
to love cage
despite
all that bullshit

1979

i'm riding
in the back of
my mother's beige
volkswagen beetle
sucking on apple
flavored now and laters
but in my mind
that was all one word
mellowing out
to john denver
singing to annie
telling her she
fills up his senses

off-white chuck taylors
jordache jeans
white t-shirt
long blue sleeves
my name ironed on
across the back
wondering how strangers
who spoke to me
already knew my name
rockin my good-haired
afro, pick folded up
in my back pocket
my wallet on
the other side
superfluously flush
with two dollars and
a library card

on our way to

dairy queen for a
footlong with chili
or a soft-serve dipped
in chocolate
after blowing my
allowance at the
comic book store
on limestone, a hole
in the wall that
smelled like dust
and fresh ink
leaving with my
stack of heroes
wrapped in brown paper

it was saturday afternoon
fresh off my
cartoon marathon
herculoids and space
ghost still on
my mind or that
chilled out chick
skating in a figure
eight, blowing my
mind, telling me
if i turn it on its
side it spells out
infinity

but i'm
in the back seat
of my mom's
beige volkswagen beetle
singing at the top
of my voice that
the devil went
down to georgia
and he was looking
for a soul to steal
but i'm bad, bad

leroy brown
and i'm leaving on a
jet plane, i don't
know when i'll
be back again

we roll into
the whistle stop pop
shop, where I get
my discount, orange
and grape soda fix
bottled while i watch
then it's back
to the car
because it's 1979
and you can
ring my bell

faster

we appear
as if fresh from
the otherworld
like mephistopheles
in our seven-league
boots overtaking faust
as though draped
in the falcon
cloak of freyja
laced into the
shoes of vidarr or
the winged sandals
of hermes knowing
that we are
somehow inherently
faster

we do not have
a costume ring into
which we have secreted
a shrunken, friction resistant suit
with a lightning bolt
across the chest
nor are we endowed
with an invisible aura
that frees us from the
inevitable grasp of
quantum physics
we come costumed
in knee-high socks
beneath the
shortest shorts ever made
a faded star wars

t-shirt, wrapping our
pre-hormonal frame
all arms and legs, our
shadow stylized by a
perfectly combed
natty halo smelling
like tcb or royal crown
with a challenge
on our lips

let's race

our super powers
had not been bestowed
by a chemical accident
an active mutant gene
or a magic word whispered
behind a recreation vehicle
but by brand new sneakers

brand. new. sneakers.

so we must have been faster
right?

you probably had
those keds, those pony racers
tretorn nylites, k-Swiss classics
those converse all-stars?

maybe you rocked
those pumas, those filas
nike all-courts or cortez
you were probably
in that addidas money crew
with your stan smiths, rod lavers
your matchplays, samoas
your superstars, or dragons

god forbid you had those suede gazelles

18

i didn't grow
up wearing hundred
dollar sneakers
mine were white
$6
chuck taylor's but
i knew i was
faster, and my
mama loved me

there was no
sneaker cleaner
protector or polish
they went in
the wash, propped
against baseboard
heaters to dry

but they were
brand new
which meant
we had to be faster
right?
ready to race you
to prove it

even if you'd
beaten us
ninety-nine times
old records were
going to be
washed away along
with the memory of
past defeats because
you were a super villain
an arch nemesis
losing was always
in your future

19

we couldn't get
out of the car
fast enough, looking
for you so we
could set the
record straight
because you hadn't
made that trip
yet, you were
still rockin those
old, broke down
loose-lace joints

you were going
down, with the
whole complex
watching because
i had on my new-news
my wonder twin powers
had been activated
so i had
to be faster

right?

virtuoso

we entered the arcade
together, but in
parallel universes

the quantum mechanics
of up and down
quarks, the dance
of hadrons with leptons
exposed the curvature
of the universe
as we crossed the
threshold onto
musty carpet
a dimly lit world of
cartoonish blips and bleeps
adolescent hormones
and the clinking
dulcimer tones of
falling quarters greeted us

it was
a casino for
the under-aged set

in my pocket
universe, coins
spilled from my
pants into an
endless progression
of console slots, indicated
by the varied and
sundry muted pings
or chimes accompanied by
flashing lights that
yelled two words at

me, over and over
like an off ramp
sign for skateboards

press start

i played with avarice
an unbecoming abandon
of gyrating joysticks
the click and
clack of buttons
all showered in
the withering song
of dying players
i was the perfect
mark, a loser made
for the short con
you unplugged at
night, the kind
of kid who made
up their profit
margins while insuring
that a mother somewhere
would be befuddled
that i had lost
my entire allowance
who was considering
whether my comic books
were a gateway drug

but not her first born

tim was the
kid they had
nightmares about
the savant, the anointed
one, a digital assassin
who for hours
ruled a world
of light and sound

racing ms. pac-man
around and around
and around the grid
with the calm
of a trappist monk
racking up extra lives
like a bodhisattva
gathering a congregation
roundabout him to
watch him attain
perfection, while they hoped
to find enlightenment
all on the back
of a single quarter
quitting when he
got tired or it
was time to go
but never, ever
because the ghosts
made him

when we left
on our way
back to the
bright light of
reality, rejoining
the real world
emerging from that
black hole into
our dimension
i would smile
because he was
my big brother
and he was a
virtuoso, with
a pocket full of
quarters to prove it

before the common era

before i discovered
i was black
i believed i was
beautiful
the spaulding clan's
golden-skinned child
raised in arms
made of love
with a natty halo
of thick curls
on my head

i was the protagonist
in a children's book
a prototype *brown*
neutron, justin case
episodes ending in
trips to the emergency
room because it wasn't
a cartoon but real
life, in which bones
break, and mother's
nerves fray

it was all
grades and girls
and brand new sneakers
all skateboards and
bmx bikes
dungeons and dragons
saturday morning
cartoons
until being black
came crashing in

24

like an unmasked
villain on scooby doo

but it wasn't marcus
garvey or malcolm x
they screamed at me
not pyramids, the
birth of arithmetic
or medicine
they did not spit
sanskrit, or hieroglyph
on me, not the
names of the places
human beings first
spoke the name
of God, or the cradle
that humanity crawled
out of, they did not say
nile
or
dynasty
haile selassie or
hat-shep-sut

it's all fun and games
until someone yells
nigger

they wanted me
to believe i was nothing
that the entire
evolution of my species
began on cheapside
where we have now
politely placed a
starbucks
and a fountain
for your enjoyment
over torn down

warehouses
haunted by the
echo of rattling chains
sweat that smelled
of fear, and the
footprints of monsters

but i had played
too many hands
of spades to believe
i was a coon
eaten too many
homemade rolls
to think i was
a jigaboo
heard my granddaddy
laugh too often
to accept darkie
drunk too much
sweet tea, had my
hair platted at the
beginning of the
summer too many
times, while falling
asleep sitting between
my mother's thighs
been told in sunday
school one time too many
to stand up straight
take my hands out
of my pockets
speak up and
e-nun-ci-ate
to believe that
i was a nigga

but it was that
word, shouted with
spittle as a punctuation
mark, and all the

ugliness that came
with it that ended my
age of innocence

they tried to
wash me away
in their pride
with their prejudice
until i was clear
i wasn't just me
i was black

before i discovered
i was black
i believed i
was beautiful

now
i know i am

sympathy and bandages

i blew myself up
in the summer
of 1979
i was high
on curiosity and
a sense of invincibility
the nature of combustible
gases in an otherwise
empty fuel tank
attached to a derelict truck
didn't care
anything about that

all it took
was a struck match
standing in for
an absent flashlight
and the whole thing
exploded in my face

it's a miracle
i made it to adulthood
and didn't force
my mother
to come up with
funeral expenses

when the world
stopped spinning, i
was staring up at
the sky with gravel
embedded in my
hands and a forehead
that was burning

dale, who had
begun this odyssey
alongside me, i would later recall
started running
when i struck the match
he heard the explosion
and would later tell
my brother who came home
to an empty house
that i had been blown up
to which tim responded
with tears, because that
had to mean his baby brother
was dead

it was Saturday afternoon
when i made it home
wandering into
the kitchen and just
standing there
until
my mother turned
from the stove
to find her
light brown baby
crispy

nothing above the eyes
remained
no brows, no skin, no hair
we laugh about it now
she and i
but on that Saturday
in the summer of 79
it wasn't funny
she just ran
with horror on her face
and her little
light brown baby boy

on her hip
she ran, leaving word
for the complex manager
to watch over her
oldest, she ran
to the car
then the hospital

and when we arrived
the nurses asked
what did gerald do
this time
they knew my name
i had been there before
that very summer
on several occasions
i was a
frequent flyer

i was the boy
who jumped off rooves
thrashed through overgrown
abandoned lots
raced my bike off
homemade ramps
leaped out of swings at
their apex, participated in
rock fights, i was
that kid

a fraction of an inch
lower, the doctor said
and he'd be blind
as they cleaned me
bandaged me, loved
on me
the nurses looking
at me with compassion
and irritation that
i had hurt myself

again

and though i was
a little too big for it
my mother carried me
on her hip
back to car
i know now
likely traumatized
and praying, and thanking
God, telling me she
wanted to be angry
with me, to punish me
but one look
at my sad state
of affairs
expunged me
of all the ramifications
from my actions
you see i had
a full white bandage
wrapped around my head

i knew it was
bad when everyone
in the pharmacy
looked at me like
i was about to die
the woman behind
the counter
proclaiming
"that's a sympathy bandage
if i ever saw one"

the rest of the
summer was a blur
recounting the tale
ointment, sympathy
and bandages

because we love
our children
too

now imagine
if i had been
murdered
by a cop

liver and lima beans

it was 1980
we had moved
to the suburbs and
some fool
had told my mother
that liver

was good for you

i promise you
i tried
i really did

ketchup, steak sauce
worcestershire and all
but it was vile
it was like
walking to the gallows
with your tongue

the salad and roll
didn't help
and for some
ungodly reason
had we done something wrong
i thought?
she gave us
lima beans on
the side

had someone told her
love
was torture?
was this what it meant

to live
in the suburbs?

now
i love my mother, more
now than then
as i look back
through time
i know
she was trying
to raise her boys well
but
to this day
i still hate liver
and lima beans

especially
lima beans

canon

is just another way of saying you miss
1950

we
still hear the rattle
of rusted chains
stained with the blood
of our mothers
and fathers
as you drag them
to the smithy
hoping they can be repaired
    we are neither deaf nor dumb

change wong
from the sorcerer supreme's
house servant
to a valued equal
and you rush to complain
about distorting the source material
destroying the integrity
of the story
but we know
what the real problem is
the one you think
we can't see
how the links
in that slaver's chain
are beginning to break
how you cherish
being the only hero
in the game
and the privilege
that comes with the cape

how you look back on 1950 fondly

say miles morales
should be the next
spider-man
or turn mary jane watson
from becky to black
you lose your mind
in the comments
anonymous behind an avatar
a fake name
filled with fake bravado
but real fear
because you see an
impending apocalypse
the end of days
a loss of your gold plated
mediocrity
as the chains
that restrain
the whole brown world
start to buckle
and fall away

it shocked me
when i landed
the tardis
laced up my chucks
threw on my
faded star trek tee
and stepped out on tatooine
out of all the worlds
where racists abide
i did not think
they lived on
planet nerd
i thought in a galaxy far
far away, just past
the twilight zone
where the brave will live

forever
in the time vortex
going where no man
has gone before
where we know fear
is the mind killer
where wonder woman
is as strong as superman
and the most powerful
green lantern that ever lived
was black
that there would be
no place for white supremacy
privilege or fragility
    i thought we were better than that

but you laugh
your racial hysterics off
play it down
with a hidden frown
hoping we won't see
just how afraid
you really are
it's just a comic
only a film
nothing to see here
just us fans
craving an allegiance
to how it's always been
you know
long live the canon
but that's real
thin
we see you
still stained
with that original
sin
wrapped up in
your greed and

gluttony
you want it all
every seat
every job
every honor
every ring
every shield
every cape
every first place in line
every corner office
every endowed department chair
every thing, every time
every where

so buckle in
because it's not over
we are just about
to begin
tearing down your monuments
colorizing your photos
making room
on mount rushmore
and when
we're through
with the red, white
and blue
there'll be some
black in it
too
every thing you've ever
held out of reach
every polished little gem you've
hidden
every seat you've reserved
every secret password you've uttered
that we've never heard
will all be laid to rest
because 1950
is dead

i'm sick

(for all the people like me who kinda sorta want to be left
alone ... kinda)

lay
the china bowl
filled with soup
surrounded
by a phalanx of saltines
softly
at the door
and walk away

don't turn on
the lights
don't ask me
how i feel
i'm sick
    and i'm not good at it

i can hit
a tiny white ball
with its shiny hexagonals
for dimples
with an odd shaped club
from hundreds of yards away
high
into the wind
shaping it left
around a tree
making it stop
on the number
nestling
next to that
small hole
    but i'm not good at this

i can dazzle you
with an exegetical brew
showing you
the hiphil clue
see these lepers
four
outside the city door
of starving Samaria
said to themselves
if we go into the city
we die
but if we stay here
we die still
so, let's go
to the enemy's camp
they can only kill us
but maybe we'll live
and when they scrounged
around and found
the camp
empty
but its treasures
there for the taking
it was the
hiphil form
of the verb
in the verse
telling the reader
it was just God doing
the thing
    but i'm not good at this

i understand
you are only
trying to make sure
i don't die
it's just that
i'm sick
so i need you

to go away
    just don't go far

run the bath water
change
the fever kissed
sheets
run to the pharmacy
for a witches brew
but don't turn on
the lights
leave the curtains
closed
and stop asking me
how i feel
you already know
just let me sleep
leave me alone
i'm sick
    and i'm not any good at it

i will respond
eventually
i will apologize
if i hurt
your feelings
i will show you
that your effort
is appreciated
when this
impolite invasion
of my body is past
and has abated
but
at the moment
i feel like
my body
is the site
of the battle
of Nagashino

my veins
the plains
of Shitaragahara
as the forces
of Takeda Katsuyori
storm the castle walls
of my momentary
immunal deficiencies

so
for now
turn off the stars
tuck the mountains
under the bed
pour out the oceans
from
where they lay
take that rainbow
down
from over my head
and
leave me alone
let me sleep
stop bothering me
just go away
 but not too far in case i need something

i'm sick

an alien axiom

if i
was to fly by
at 300 million meters
per second, in my
shinny supa fly snuka
space ship, and it was
equipped, with a
hypospray that
cured cancer
the sun in a cup
at room temperature
the answer to greenhouse gas
and a pass on mortality

but then i looked
down, and all around
saw how you treated
black and brown folks
wouldn't i just
fly on by
since i'm green

same street

(for baltimore)

it's the same street
all the world over
only the names
have been changed
to protect your
delusion

yeah, you cheered
and jeered, from your
couch, with potato chip
crumbs on your wife beater
because it was Ahmad
in the street
throwing rocks and his socks
at Abdul, screaming
fuck Assad and his mob
because, you know
that was right, and good
and proper, because, you
know, freedom was on
the line, and they were
fighting for the soul of
their country and long may
that shit reign

but let Junebug hit
that street, that same
muthafuckin street, with Big
Tim, and Little Man
with their Jordan's half
laced and their pants hanging
down, let DeShawn and
Demetrius, throw rocks

44

at Connor, Bradley, and Joe
over on M. L. K or Jefferson street
right across from the
liquor sto
screaming fuck the police
and no justice, no peace
then all of a sudden
it's a travesty, a got damn shame
because those aren't the names
of freedom fighters

just niggers

pride and prejudice

how do you
watch your roommate
cover himself in horror
like it's lotion
and say nothing

are we lost in
a dark wood
are these beasts
we cannot escape
are we waiting to be
rescued by virgil
is this the seventh
circle of dante's inferno
maybe it's just
that you think you
don't have to carry
your conscience or
humanity in your wallet

how do you have
breakfast with timothy
mcveigh, watch
him put on terror
like it's a t-shirt
and you don't call
someone, anyone to
say evacuate the building

your silence is
so profound that my
eardrums are bleeding
from the deafening volume
of your apathy
where is your heartbeat

or are you a vampire
who only feeds on blood
don't you have a
reflection in the mirror
or do the magnetic
letters on your
refrigerator spell out
i don't give a damn

how do you watch
tv with ted kaczynski
while he puts postage
on his packages during
the commercial breaks
and say nothing
have you watched that
much fox news
or do you put your
soul in a drawer when
you come home
maybe you were
raised by monsters
and have become one too

your silence is choking
the joy out of the world
like hands around the
neck of someone's child
someone's mother
someone's lover
yes, we have those too
have you listened to
that much talk radio
that you would
share a beer on
the back porch with
jared loughner, listening
to his conspiracy theory
the sound of him
parroting alex jones'

47

insanity while cleaning
his assault rifle
and you say nothing
you don't call the
congresswoman's office
to tell them a demon
is descending on them

are you a fallen
angel, a shadow or shade
are you a beast with
a number etched in
your head, or a savage
unused to the conventions
of polite society
how could you live
with animals dressed in
human skin and never
say a mumbling word

is it pride
or
prejudice

even as we speak

there are six
year olds
now living, even
as we speak
who have only
ever known
that a black man
rules the world

what dreams might they be dreaming

maybe they are
dreaming
like imhotep
who, upon
the death of
king zoser
looked over
the mastabas
those sacred
burial mounds
and dreamed for
the first time
that they
should be built
on the curve
of an hypotenuse
rather than the
inelegant vertices
of a square
leaving, *as sahra al-kubra*
the great desert

irrevocably marked by trigonometry ratios
made of limestone aimed toward the
heavens

there are
first graders, even
as we speak
carrying their
fat, red, eraserless
pencils in their
back pockets, who
have only ever
known that
a black man
rules the world

what walls might they be preparing to tear
down

maybe they will
devour disciplines
whole like
that wild-haired
postal clerk
who scribbled
his madness
on bits of paper
during his lunch break
or on the weekends
who first believed
that time wasn't
fixed to your
wrist but was
dependent
on when you
were where you
were and how
fast you were
traveling when
you got there

leaving three letters, held apart by a
qualifier
squared, onto our collective memory

there are
tricycle riders
with their
shoelaces hanging
on for dear life
building forts
made out of
sheets in their
bedrooms, even
as we speak
who have only ever
known that
a black man
rules the world

what wonders might they have in mind

thank god
they don't have
our hang ups

you can see it
in that moment
in the White House
turned black
when the light
in their eyes
flickers to life
just above
the lollipop they
are sucking on
as they watch
one of their
tiny tribe touch
his hair to see
if it's like
their own

missing malcolm

i wish Malcolm
had been carrying
a 9
in the small
of his behind
an autobiography
is not
enough

i want a gray
headed
god of thunder still
sitting on olympus
in harlem, a slim lapeled
suit with a skinny tie
and black wingtips
the patron saint
of public intellectuals
and black presidents

i wanted his
prolegomena
to any future histrionics
to sit in his
intro to philosophy
class, to sign
up for his office
hours so that
i could go over
my paper on semiotics
and its impact
on how we
view the self
with him

to be his
teaching assistant
bringing him his
turkish coffee
first thing
every morning

to have him wholly
surgically eradicate the word
nigga
from our vocabulary
like a drone
strike over Kandahar
have it appear
right there
on the front
page of the
Times
knowing that would
be the last word
on it that
we would
have to have
a funeral
burying it
without complaint
that we would
narrow our eyes
at anyone who
tried to call us that
because it was
dead, terrorist
marked off the
kill list dead
announced by the
White House press
secretary dead
in a potters field
in a pine box
without a headstone

paid for by
the state dead

because Malcolm said so

i wish Malcolm
had been carrying
a 9 in the
small of his
behind that
day at the Audubon

i don't want
a tshirt
i want a collected
works, which i
got signed at the Strand
after his, an evening with
Malcolm, reading
i don't want
a poster
i want him
firmly planted
in a think tank
in harlem
named after Du Bois
with a statue of
Frederick Douglass
in the lobby

i wish
Malcolm had a
9 up against
his behind when
that fool yelled
"get yo hand outta my pocket"

interrogatory

if
our black bodies
were out of quantum phase
with your
hands, lips, and bullets

if
our music
vibrated at a frequency
your ears could not
devour

if
our recipes
were written in a dialect
your culinary imaginations
could not
consume

if
all of our us
were transported
to a planet
circling
a distant star

what then?

original sin

(for amerika)

descendant of thieves
desperately clinging
to your fading
privilege

the crime
you are most
guilty of
is believing
there is only
enough room
in the sunshine
for you

and then
doing whatever it took
to make it true

may you remain
unforgiven

a hundred miles and still running

(On the occasion of watching an unarmed black man crawl away from police in the hopes of survival)

1622

the sun is in my face
my heart pounds like the low thump-thump of the drum-drum
i can feel the heat of the sand beneath my feet, the salty spray
of the bahari on my face
there are strange, pale men, covered in hair, who smell of death
at my back, and i am running
i have heard the stories, told
when the fires burn low and the children sleep
if they catch you they will rip you out of the world
so even when the net falls over me, i fight and bite and claw
until darkness descends over my eyes, because i do not want to go

1743

the moon swells overhead
my heart is pounding like the hard clang-ga-clang of a hammer on shackles
i can feel the cool earth beneath my feet
and the warm southern air on the blood dripping down my back
there are white men, covered in hair, who smell of rum, rape, and death
behind me, and i am running
i have heard the stories, told
when the candle's flickering light is low, while the master and his men are drunk or asleep
of the beautiful world our babas and mamas were ripped out of
so as the barking, snarling dogs draw closer to me, i resolve to fight, bite, and claw
until darkness descends over my eyes, because i'm not going back

1921

the sky, overhead, is bright with the reflected light from the fires that rage below
my heart is pounding like the bang of my office door slamming shut
i can feel the rumbling stampede of hundreds of people on the street beneath my feet
there are white men, covered in hair, who smell of jealousy, cheap whisky, and death
behind me, and i am running
with my family, through the neighborhoods we built
we have told our children the stories
once we raised the buildings for their schools, their homes, banks, and grocery stores
of the beautiful world their ancestors were ripped from and we recreated here
so as our city burns down around us, set on fire by those angered by our prosperity, we resolve
to fight, bite, and claw if we must
until the last embers of our burning world fall into darkness, because we will not stop

2016

the sun blazes through my windshield
my heart pounds like the 808 kick drum-drum-drum from
the Public Enemy song blaring out of my speakers
as i leap from the car, i can feel the heat radiating from the asphalt beneath my feet
the sound of the city fades into awful silence in my ears
there are white men, dressed in indifference, who smell of fear, privilege, and hate
behind me, and i am running
praying someone with a cellphone is watching
i've seen the other stories, where they couldn't keep the video from getting out
of how they rip black men and women, even children, out of the world
in cold blood and get away with it
so when i hear them fire their guns, and the searing pain knocks me off my feet
i crawl, fighting to live, biting my lip, clawing at the ground
until my vision gets dark, because somewhere deep in my soul
i want to be free

star spangled

my legs
are not weak
they do not shake
or tremble
they are as strong
as my grandmother's back
bowed but not broken
over
an ironing board
in her room
in the attic
of a white person's house

my ears
are not plugged with cotton
the sound of injustice
is not drowned out
by beats and rhymes
i hear your drums
your fifes
the *ratta tat tat*
of your egregious
celebration
though they do ring
from the sound of gunfire
  and the shouts of
  all lives
  mattering

my eyes
are not shrouded
by the brim
of a red, white, and blue
baseball cap

an american hijab
made from sweatshop fabric
purchased at hobby lobby
mass produced to make
america white again
they are not covered by scales
i can see your wanton abandon
your sacred cows
fattened on genetically modified
feed
i am not lost
in the antilles
of your fragile emotions
searching for a compromise
between the two souls
of a native not native son
   though why you are worried
   about an invisible man
   you refuse to see
   puzzles me

your bugle sounds
clearly
your flag waves
with the crisp snap
of a coffin cover
your masses throng
adoringly
as they always have
blindly obedient
to a nonexistent *manifesticated*
destiny
rendering a pledge
to a body politic
suffering from dysmorphia
worshipping an idol
seen only as a reflection
in a funhouse mirror
stained with blood
being interpreted

by minds drenched
in privilege
like it's a natural
hormone
secreted by whiteness glands
high on delusion
from sniffing indulgence
with rolled up hundreds
lost to the ravages
of a star-spangled alzheimer's
   you have refused
    to have diagnosed
    or treated

because you have to want
to get well
which would require
remembering your sins
the ones the rest of us
have to live with

my legs
are not weak
neither
is my soul
though
it is tired
which is why
i will not
stand
for your fucking anthem

prolegomena to any
future metaphysics

where
should we lay
our grief-vances?
along the empty street
on the steps
of the house
you've abandoned?

because
it's not your debt
you say
and we no longer
suffer
while you collect
the interest
on the bones
of our mothers
and fathers
with a spring
in your step
and the horror
of your familial sins
is written
in our dna

to whom
should we address
our petition
for redress?
should not the voices
that cry out
from their graves
be heard?

do they not
deserve

their day
in the sun?

you hide
in broad daylight
like a child
playing hide and seek
but we are not
indulgent parents
or mistaken friends
we are the descendants
of the aggrieved
the inheritors
of their chains

just because
you renamed them
does not make a collar
easier to wear
nor the air
in a prison
easier
to breathe

you cannot escape
the reckoning
by changing your address
with the postmaster

because

it's because your
bias is wrapped around
my neck like an
nypd chokehold
a bias that's as
dangerous and contagious
as ebola because you
won't even acknowledge
you have it, and you
break quarantine
like the rules don't
apply to you

it's because your
ignorance is sitting so
heavily on my chest
like a tulsa county sheriff's knee
an ignorance that's as debilitating
as a mandatory minimum occupation
for a privately run prison
all the more dangerous
because judges become check
out clerks, scanning black
bodies and asking whether
you want paper
or plastic body bags

it's because your
silence, your offensive
malodorous silence, sucks
all the air out of the room
like a discharged 357
mistaken for a taser
by a white man on safari in
oklahoma, empties the air

out of a brown man's lungs
all the more insulting
because you think
it's ok to play starsky
and hutch, expecting me
to be huggy bear

that's why
i can't breathe

welfare

your privilege is
as invisible to you
as the air
you breathe
but that does not
stop you
from taking up
all the oxygen
in the room
it's like knowing
you can't lick
your elbow
or sneeze
with your eyes open

why would you even care?

your world
is shrink-wrapped
though unlabeled
passed down to you
generationally
over the counter
in broad daylight
but in a store
the rest of us
can't shop in
but you didn't notice
how white the aisles were
how male
how empty
like knowing
the letters on your zipper
stand for

yoshida kogyo kabushikigaisha

why would you be bothered?

you are insulated
like your daddy
and his before him
by the suffering
of others
wrapped up and padded
against all damage
with the hunger
sadness, loss
and desperation of people
browner than you
in a package
made for travel
by special courier
from your nurses lullaby
to your funeral choir's
requiem

and you aren't aware
your seat
is in first class?

like the psalmist said
lift up
your fucking head
o ye gates
and be ye lifted up
ye everlasting doors
and the king of glory
shall come in
to save you
from all that
unearned privilege

take one breath
that isn't

67

vacuum packed
lay down your
obliviousness
as if it were
gluten
or some other heresy
take off your
headphones
   the ones you think
   give you a ghetto pass
   to hiplandia

   do you care
   about anything
   besides
   how your jeans fit?

that extra social
height
might be as
imperceptible to you
as the predators
in our neighborhoods
like the out of control cops
twenty percent interest rates
check cashing companies
but it's as clear
to the rest of us
as your denial
and we are
tired
of giving you
welfare

zero percent financing

on november 9th
i began
trading in my white folks
some of the ones
i had
were broken
i thought they were
decent
but it turned out
they were lemons
with manufacturing flaws
not road worthy
burdened with the kinds
of damage
that does not show up
on a test drive

socio-economic racists
powder coated
with white supremacy
on their frames
baked in
under the paint
where you can't see it
until you have
an accident
or an unarmed
black person gets
murdered by cops
engines so used
to running
on so much
high octane privilege
they burn oil
spewing smoke

and noise
in the place of
decency and justice

so i've been
trading them in
on newer models
self-effacing
electric
aware of their
price tags
aiming to make
the world better
first, by spouting
less gas into the air
second, by knowing
when to turn off
favoring mileage
over promises

do yourself
a favor
get you some
new white folks
i'm not sure
the ones you have
can be saved
or if it's even
worth trying
especially since
you can get
new ones with
zero percent
financing

the antichrists

(1 John 2:18b - so now many antichrists have come.)

a brown-skinned fire
burned brightly
for the briefest
moment
on a barren stretch
of time
in an effort
to rekindle
the faded embers
of the human soul
striking the sparks
in his own
blood

the white church
has taken pains
to put it out
like a smoked cigarette
crushed
into
an ash-filled tray
in a ford pickup
with a war on christmas
bumper sticker
on the back
destined
to be emptied
out the window
like their souls
while they nod
at children
in cages
and listen to mad men
reminisce
about simpler times
when being soulless
was easier

71

passover

(on the occasion of another non-election night in the bluegrass)

kentucky still
practicing that
self-immolation
with a side of
grits
like a green tomato
slice
rolling in cornmeal
throwing itself
into a black
iron skillet
like falling off
a stolen tractor
during a hayride
driven by
a used car salesman

somebody
with a half-smoked
cig said it

good night and
good luck

bless your heart

i don't remember
where i heard it
first
it was just
in the air
like please, thank you
and ma'am

it's that tart
piece of lemon
floating on a
white frosty layer
of glaze
in the sweet ice tea
it's that extra inch
of meringue
on the brown
sugar pie
it was the big smile
wrapped around
a cruel lie

you see, down here
where the ale eight is cold
and the a la mode is warm
where cole slaw
and baked beans
on the side
of fried catfish
is the law
we don't scream
kiss my ass

we like to pour molasses

on our consternation
lap it up
with a biscuit

nobody does it better
than a saccharine
sanguine sara
a how do you do
sally mae, anna bell
patricia faye or abbie gail
with her gum poppin
and her hips rockin
to the side
with a manicured hand
perched
just so
on a hip
curved like
a granny smith
apple

you see, down this way
where the grass
is blue
between the corn bread
and the corn puddin
with homemade rolls
and collard greens
chased down with
five
berry
pie
we don't holla
dumb motherfucker or
take the lord's name
in vain

we like to spread butter
all over our dissatisfaction
eat it toasted

maybe with a little
strawberry preserve

so listen close
or you might mistake
the smile
for a grin
or the curse
for a blessing

because
down here
where the whisky
is bourbon
and the koolaid
is diabetes sweet
we don't yell
fuck you

we like to smother it
and cover it
with gravy
until it's running
over the sides

down here
we smile
we wave
and say

bless your heart

the destroyer of worlds

(for the borrowers of books)

i will not
loan my books
to the goddess

Kali said
i will devour
them

with a gleam
of delight
in her eyes
her six arms
outstretched
the destroyer said
she would take
them as tribute
but they
would not return
whole

she said
she would peel
back their skin
and with many-fingered
glee
she would crack
their spines
sucking out their
marrow with
a coffee stirrer

standing astride
the world with
the remains

of bound pages
in her tantric hands
stained
battered
emaciated
the Black Goddess of Dakshineswar
the destroyer of worlds
said she would
leave them in
her wake
like broken ships
scattered along a sanskrit shore

the Slayer of Raktabija
drunk on the
blood of verses
with paragraphs dripping
from her fangs
dances among the
corpses of tattered tomes

she does not
promise
resurrection to those
who worship
at her temple
only a kind
of reincarnation
a pity induced restitution
wrapped in infatuation
for the loss
of loved ones

so while
i love those
who love words
who love the taste of them
who love how they smell in the morning

i cannot

loan the goddess
my books

Kali said
i will devour them

shipwreck

who knew
the sea was so full?

crippled ships
lurching past ports of call
but never making for land
listing in the wind
     mistaking the current for fate

pirate galleys
luxury schooners
war ships of the line
at a distance
     leaky scows with tattered sails up close

broken hulls
shattered rudders
confusion at the helm
flying no colors to speak of
     they no longer have anchors

board
at your peril

circadia

thick curls
long and straight
freckled face
or smooth
thin or curvy
she has a thousand faces
but it's always
the same woman

she motions for me
to join
her
barefoot
on a thick dirt
path

when i arrive
she grabs my hand
like it's the last one
in the whole world
and laughs like
she gargles with music
pulling me down
the path
into a glorious wood
i remember
her dress
covered
in daisies
and her skin
in stars like glitter
the woods
the hills
the trees
i know

it's home
where the grass
is blue
the whiskey
brown
when i wake
it's not her dress
or her hair
or her laughter
i remember most

it's how she held
my hand
like it was
the only thing
keeping her
from falling off
the world

kentucky love

you're the corner
piece of cornbread
the red onion
in my
brown beans
the piece
of cake
with
my name
on it

the ketchup
on my fries

the new laces
in my boots
the patches
on my sleeves
the ink under
my skin

you're the cuff
in my levi's

great depression

a soup kitchen
is not
responsible
for a full
heart
even if
you only have
empty feelings
at home

besides
they're closed
at night

feeding sisyphus

i
no longer
shower likes
on human beings
like confetti
every time
they throw
a one person
parade

it
feeds their
want
a buffet
of empty calories
ending in
obese souls
and clogged empathy
in need of
bypass surgery

and who
can afford
the copay
on that?

dreamcatcher in the rye

a vision of havana is stuck in my dreamcatcher
of you closing down an open-air cantina with me
making empty glasses of white rum and lime, sweet
with sugar and moonlight on their rims
we are sitting at a too small table while a guitar weeps
the smell of cuban cigars blown softly around our heads
by a warm breeze off the *atarés*, ruffling the pleats
in your summer skirt and the flower petals in your hair
there is something primordial about the twinkle in your eyes

paris is reflected on the shiny coin i throw into the *la danse*
in the 13th arrondissement, though it's not april and you
are smiling, because we have come to crumple our ennui up
in pastry paper, leaving it among the remains of croissants
and empty espresso cups for the waiter to dispose of
we are expats, wrapped in scarves, haunted by the ghost of Sartre
you hold my hand as we snub the Mona Lisa in favor of fromage
and bits of baguette while we stroll the Luxembourg gardens
and there is something eternal about the sparkle of your smile

the first star of the night gleams as brightly as my thought of us
alone on a beach, *la digue* island calling from deep on the indian ocean
white sand covers the red polish on your toes, the sky blue water still
clinging to your skin, your belly button peeking through your sheer
monachino
mischief is in the air as we light a bonfire and sip mojitos in the dark
we are all alone, holding each other on the lip of the ocean, like its
the very edge of the world, as if God is starting over with just the two of us
and there is something aboriginal about the sound of your laughter

and when we are gone, the remains of our love, like photographic negatives
echoes in caves, the light of a distant star finally reaching the earth, will live

elegy in blue

shave a layer of skin from your nose
because spite needs to be seasoned
sprinkle it like parmesan over the ashes you are dining on

light up your monuments to the broken promises of your fleeting grace
in varying hues of white, to honor night fallen on *champs de mars*
while colored tines cloaked in winding sheets garnish cooling boards in red
along the tigris, mid-mediterranean, the hard pan dirt of tattered *baga*
where brown bodies, unbreathing, lay their bullet-riddled heads, unremarked
upon

where does apathy go to die, i wonder, is there a map that shows the way?
or can i barter with you to add a wrinkle to your smooth forehead
must i call up Ayangalu from the grave to beat the drums
the djembe, dundumba, and sangban, or the griots to play us a woe
brown bodies, unbreathing, lay their battered heads on a hard pillow of your
silence

would that miles or monk could wander into an elegy for you
wrap that sound around the cellophane dissonance you wear like a double-
breasted
overcoat, have your tailor hem your indifference so it hangs to the knee or
breaks at the shoe
because brown bodies, unbreathing, lay stacked like wood, on the fields of
abandon

and they are just as deserving of an elegy etched in every single hue,
especially blue

the kiss

you taste like
tomorrow

a warm
beignet-sweet
promise of proustian evenings
sprinkled
with powdered sugar
wrapped in cellophane
chased with mason jars
teased by wine
instead of properly ravished
by old enough
scotch
it was there
all of it
on your tongue
as the sound of your
heartbeat
played on the phonograph
in the corner
of
my wanting you
sitting, impeccably, in place
on an eamesian sensibility
with four legs
just off the staircase
curved like your lips
leaving me room
to lean in
only far enough
that the kiss-me
was left

up to you

dizziness
hung in the air
like the drifting smoke
of burnt incense
patiently waiting
to be inhaled
when we came up
for air
but i was lost
in the feel
of your hand
laying lightly
on my cheek
the hint
of your breath
on my chin
as
a thousand years
passed by while you
nuzzled your nose
against mine

you taste like
tomorrow

breezes soft
as your skin
wet summer rain
and the sun
on my face
all that resting
on your lips
as you parted them
hesitantly at first
before turning playful
until it finally became
a hint of you
wanting me

as you tilted
your head
just so
leaving me
awash
in you
in the lasting
taste of you
in my mouth
drifting in the sweet echo
of
your laughter
off
the crumbling walls
of my yesterday
the beauty
of your mind
at work
like
a play
i have not seen
a book
i am longing
to read
as you
leaned lightly
against me while the night
burned away
as if it was
a lit candle
i
could not stop
slowly disappearing

i am left adrift
in imagining
the purple haze
of
a morning sky
well-worn jeans

around your curved
hips
the sound
of
milk frothing
while espresso drips
from
sparkling fonts
in the kitchen
at dawn
ice rattling around
in vodka filled
shakers
at the evening
of the day
tonic
for you
extra olives for me
as i gaze
into
the wise
in your eyes

but since i
may not twist time
to my will
like a piece
of
lemon peel perched
on the rim
of
my glass
it ends
that all too brief moment
on the other side
of your lips

and though it
has passed
 into

the well
of my memories
know
it is not far off
i am pleasantly
haunted
by the feel
of your lips
against mine

because you
taste like
tomorrow

at least
that
is what i imagine

a description in muse

you are a wandering apostrophe
a thousand miles away
the salt on the rim of the milky way
a sweet and sour comet
roaming the galaxy
the cool side of a pillow at the morning
end of my dreams
the purr of my engine
in the curve of a joy ride
the last page of my favorite book
the last time my heart will sigh
a wildish thing to be braved not tamed

a period on the last line around my eyes before they
fade

lunar interlude in c minor

meet me on the backside of the moon
take a ride on the tail of this hundred year comet
i'll be right here waiting when the sun falls down

wear your favorite dress
made of starlight and dream
the one that falls just below the need

bring a bottle of rye nestled beneath your breast
dab a little behind your ear where my tongue will rest
sipping it from your belly button on my way down to
your nest

meet me on the backside of the moon
just past the sea of tranquility
i'll still be here when the sun begins to rise

we can say things after

when the carpenters
won't let you sleep

have you ever
come half awake
so that you still
have strings tied
to the toes
of your dream

you can
lick it, taste it
play with it
like it's pancake batter
on your fingertips

in my dream
you are not broken
and *close to you*
plays in the background
as you straddle me

i recall wondering
as i recognize
who you are
if you left
the you i adored
on the salon floor
or maybe you
just think you did

for some reason
she is still singing
just like me
they long to be

close to you
like a ghost
haunting the attic
looking
for the rest
of my rem sleep
in a dust-covered trunk

i have
the oddest epiphany
that i am not
romeo
and you are
desdemona

though
i remember
this is just
a dream, i know
i'll have to
revisit that later
and you are not
here, with your legs
wrapped around me
and your breath
on my face

a ceiling fan spins
as i look past
your light brown shoulder
i realize, in that
brief moment
that the soundtrack
i have grown up with
has saved me
from pretty
disguised as love

and when i wake
you will still

be broken
but i will find
that song
the one reverberating
off the bedroom walls
of this dreamscape
and play it
something about *why
do birds sing*
mixed with dream-want
and the memory
of the sweetness
of having you

i will realize
to my chagrin
that i am burdened
with the distant echoes
of too many
seventies love songs
to sleep unenchanted

finally
like the end
of a sonnet
i am awake
with a taste
for you
still
on my hazy lips

contemplating
whether to tell you
or just
go back
to sleep

on pointe

i can tell
by the way
you twirl your *meisterstück*
between your long
manicured fingers
that you point
your toes

painted purple
red
or french tipped

parce que ce serait cliché

freshly-shaved legs
without hose
beneath a flared
polka dot skirt
i am entwined
in your smile
which promises
scattered blankets
and heavy breathing
as if we are running
late
for the *hiram bingham*
from cuzco
to machu picchu

i can tell
by the way
you put on
your lipstick
that you are noisy
naughty
and you pointe

i think of you

gripping my sheets
your eyes wide
with surprise
at the size
of my investment
in our
conjugation

i am not shocked
as the smell
of shalini
drifts up from the sweat
that trickles
between your breasts
down to your navel
like the *seneca*
south, past your
spruce knobs
or how
your fingernails slide
down my back
leaving a trace of you
like a trail
winding through
red river gorge

i glance
over my shoulder
as you close your eyes
surrendering
to the dissolution
of our ids into
we go together
like peanut butter
on sweet apple slices
and just as i suspected
you are pointing
your toes

because
you are
a fucking
lady

great expectations

some may
consider
the greatness
of my expectations
a starry-eyed
conceit
that i am
sitting in an
existential cold
wrapped
in a warm
blanket woven
with
strands of naïveté
with holes
in it

but i believe
that while we
breathe
there is hope
that we
who search
among the rubbish
of a wasted landscape
littered with the
unmoving corpses
of lives unlived
hearts unloved
dreams denied
that somewhere
among the refuse
we can find
who we were
born to be

i can see
your tears
from here
your deep
bottomless
yearning for
a pure moment
an honest encounter
with that deepest
of mysteries
not the who
or what, or where
the jones at the
outdoor cafe along
the *avenue des champs-élysées*
those things that
seem so interchangeable
but your most
inner hunger for
an answer to
the quintessential
interrogative
the purest of
the inquisitives

why

i can see
your yearning
to reach out
as you pass
other unspeaking
beings
who float by
you daily
like ghosts in
a graveyard sitting
at the end
of all time

and space
like a road
to nowhere, i
see the want
in you, that
indecent urge to
accost a stranger
with your joy
or sadness, to
blunder past the
pedantic pleasantries
of empty greetings
and salutations so
that for once you
will experience
an authentic emotion
an emphatic interaction
with another, but
you let the moment
pass
like the shade
that comes and goes
with the
cloud that passed
before the sun
because you
are afraid of
disturbing
the perfunctory nature
of our ingrained
even intransigent
civilities which
doom us to an isolation
of the cruelest
kind

but be forewarned
that if you
you beautifully
singular, irreplaceably

unique point
in the universe
if you do not
brazenly
reach out against
the repressive forces
of gentility
you will die
you will die
sitting over those
same poached eggs
sipping
that same cup
of coffee
you will die
you will die
putting on that
same blue sweater
you will die
you will die
pretending you
are unique
acting out
the part of an artist
or lover
or friend while
not realizing
that you died

days ago

so rise up
from the coffin
of the fear
you lay in
walk out into the
sunlight
you shy away from
because if
you still breathe

there is hope
that you can have the life
we all so
quietly, desperately
want, but
only if you
are willing
to take it

ego trip

(on the occasion of the Affriliachian Poets 15th anniversary)

let me
walk this
thought
around your head
and
step these words
in your ear

fireflies are beetles
Immanuel Kant
never left his hometown
and this
this ain't no
ego trip

this
is where
the fire started

right here
where the ground
is black
right here

with a few
pieces of
paper and
a few pieces of
i gotta say
something
on
mouth wipes
and torn off

pieces of
sunday morning
bulletins
the back of
coffee receipts and
I need to
go to class
schedules

this is where
the fire
started
right here where
the earth
is scorched

let me walk
this thought
around your
head and
step
these words in
your ear

the Gregorian calendar
still doesn't work
Kierkegaard thought it
was somebody else
whispering to Abraham
about Isaac
and this
this ain't no
ego trip

i remember
catchin a piece
of i gotta write
this down
by the corner

getting a hold
of the hem
of its garment
and like
that woman who
fought through
the crowd to
touch God
who was out
for a
walk because she
had to

i remember
fightin through the
crowds of
already saids
not quite justifieds
why this word
here and
that phrase
there?
what do you
mean its
untitled? and
you tried to come
in here without
copies!?

we were
looking
looking in
boxes of words
like children
searching for
favorite toys
but we
were looking
for just
the right way

to just the right
say it
to play it
across the
Orpheum and Lyric
of the mind
like it was
opening night

let me
walk this thought
around your
head and
step these words in
your ear

there are
didn't do its on death row
beautiful women are the most insecure
and this
yeah this
this
ain't no
ego trip

this is where
the fire started
right here
where the
grass doesn't
grow any more

you see
once you
had it
found it
backed over it
and
wrestled it down
until you could

be sure
it wouldn't get
off the page
you had to
tell somebody
had to
tell some
body, had to tell
somebody

and
so we
came

sliding in
quietly
with a piece
of get you
high under
our coat
motioning for
those with
a sweet tooth
like ours
to meet
us in
the back

and if
we could not
get it
with out a
side dish
of
somebody else

we would
take our
scroll and
make our stroll

to that lift me
up to the next
floor
we would pile
in like
we was goin
somewhere
only it wasn't
to an up
listed on
the press me
here
no
it was a
take me up
on the wind
of somebody's
i gotta say
something

and when
the door
closed
and the hold us
here button
was pushed

we blissed
yeah
we blissed
and
nodded our heads
to a
you ain't lyin
passing the pepper
because no
matter what
anybody else had
to say
we be

poets
feeling
like the whole
universe
was two feet
by four feet
with a slidin door
and a chime
that announced
we be
here

it was right
here
where the ground
is black
and the grass
doesn't grow anymore
where the
fire started

and so
we pass this
way
and give a
we know now nod
to the then
because we
know that
Mars has water
Nietzsche went insane
but this
yeah
this right here

this ain't
no
ego trip

for norman

come, let us
gather up our
sorrow, like grandmother's yarn
strewn across the floor
in passing
and remember the Poet
we once knew

there will be memories
stained with tears
and words, paired together
like peanut butter on
sweet apple slices
seven sevens, in a
line, ya dig

we will spackle
over the cracks
his going leaves
in us, with our
favorite phrases ground
up with a bit of west
virginia dirt and bourbon
mixed into smooth paste
spread on with
old book covers

so come, let us
gather up our loss
like playing cards
strewn across the
dinner table
there are still
hands of spades and

bid whist to be played
and while we laugh
cut suits and lie
about the number
of books in our hand
let us remember
and raise a rock
glass in the
mountains of affrilachia
to the Poet
gone from among us

the one we still know

25

(an affrilachian cento)

because
part of the bluegrass
is black
seven sevens in a line
ya dig
we were raised
by women
before it was cool
some in a hospital
that no longer exists
you look like the brown one
but act like the white one

never got to see
a bird stay still
driftwood sleepy, we
had to call everyone
black we knew
do the math
'til you exist

we be poets
the riffing of
deeply enamored minds
slipping through
horizontal windows
making empty glasses
of bourbon

because
we knew how low

a back had to bend
to fill a sack
of sorrow
pushed to wish
our blackness away
or kill the landlord
that muthaphuka
but we did not
sell each other
to abandonment

because
this ain't no
ego trip
it began where
the moonlight ended
from as far as
six galaxies away

people wave
and call it community
sending charcoal smoke signals
but we said no
to this only way
they wanted to know
black people
and the babbling children
whose speech had
not yet cooled into sense

we are thick
into year twenty-five
we have endeavored
filling the streets
with a kind of
voracious, simple
yearning
because we imagined
being affrilachian
poets

Special Edition Poems

ozymandias, but no king

if
i am murdered
by whiteness
do not look
away
play
the video
a thousand times
for every door
closed in my face

if i
am murdered
by privilege
off it's leash
swearing it is
not
hatred
because it knows
tasha or dre
do not
turn your face
from the glaring
light
of my loss
press play
a million times
once
for every assumption
that they were
better than me

if i am
murdered
by Amerika
high on its red and white
do not close your eyes

replay the images
again and again
until the horror
can no longer
be escaped
by logging out

it's why
Emmett Till's
mama
left the casket
open

in the shadow of Golgotha

if they kill me
do not forgive them
in my name
do not say
it's what he would've wanted
instead
throw that yearning
on the bonfire
already burning
fuel the conflagration
until it can be seen
from *proxima centauri*
light up the night
with rage
because this shit
has to stop
and peace is not
working

if they murder me
do not hold
a press conference
offering absolution
to my murderers
do not hug
my mama
with idle hands
fuck that noise
instead
throw that spirit
on the wheel
of the world

119

in the hopes
that it will
wreck the gears
and stop its
turning
because forgiveness
is not working

if they erase me
from the world
go to war
because forgiveness
is for community
and they've never
been family

effigy

i
do not want
my image
spray painted
a hundred feet high
on the brick wall
of a tenement
in memoriam
another
cautionary tale
or veiled threat?

i
do not want
a tshirt
with my last words
emblazoned
across the chest
another sacrifice
to the unsatiated
demigods of hatred

i
do not want
a moment of silence
to remember me
a gesture as empty
as the thoughts and prayers
of mesmerized sycophants
and counterfeit
saints

i
do not want
the people
i love

grasping
for a way
to make sense
of the madness
of wannabe kings
and paupers

i
want
to live

meggido

how many
times
are we supposed
to lay out
our grievances
like biscuits
on a baking
sheet
only to have them
thrown
in the garbage
or left out
to go stale

how many times
are we
supposed to come
sit at a table
with antichrists
to politely
discuss
how you will do
nothing
but write down
our pain
on the back
of a coffee stained
napkin

how many times
are we
supposed to mourn
the ex·san·gui·na·tion
of our souls
onto hot concrete

while you nod
and promise
things will be different
if we just
give you a minute

how many minutes
are there
in two hundred
years?

times up

daddy's girl
(on the occasion of the death of erica garner)

amerika
broke
erica garner's heart
into pieces
so small
that she could
no longer
breathe

medusa in apogee

don't be
shifting sand
beneath her feet

she will
cut
her hair
like a warrior
making
a blood oath
to avenge
the broken promises
that lay scattered
at her feet

obliterating you
from the memory
of all things
like a pair
of panties
best left
where they lie
and replaced
rather than
retrieved

she will
leave you
behind
like a spent rocket
as she leaves
orbit

and i
will be waiting
to be

the other reason
your name
has died
on her tongue

i dream of frida

i lost
myself
somewhere between
your brown fingers
and toes
unable to tell
you from me
in this hot
tangle of need
and want

i am
overcome
by the smell
of sage, sweat
and sweet
wet womanhood

i stopped
at your navel
contemplating
the light sheen
of sweat from
our exertions
nestling on your
creamy skin
like dew on grass
before licking
the salty elixir of you
away
with my warm
tongue

the farther down
i went
the sweeter

you became
until the rising
exaltation
in your voice
like an orchestral
crescendo played
in ac*celerando*
telling me
to stop right there
with your hand
on my head
telling me to wait
for the train
that was cuming
followed
finally
by your
exhale
in *adagio*

the breathy sound
of you in my ear
even now
from a thousand
miles away
wakes all
of me
with the taste
of you somehow
still
on my lips
the smell of you
still
in my nostrils

my hand
slides
across the cool
sheets
and i realize

you were only here
in
my dreams

i am not a feminist

since
you don't
go to war
with
my mama
niece
and grandmother
in mind
since
y'all don't show up
when black women
need you
since
your revolution is
founding on the
proposition that
all lily's and becky's and karen's
deserve the same
privileges
their father's have

i am not a
feminist

time travel for wanna be revolutionaries

(because i went to college with you)

        if only
        you had a time
        machine
        then
        you could go back
        wake yourself up
        roll out of the bed
        you were in
        while the rest of us
        were making
        black lives
        that mattered

        maybe
        you could erase
        the timeline
        in which you were
        anti-black
        on the front page
        of the kernel
        or where you
        were just
        a clown
        trying to matriculate
        who only had room
        in his class schedule
        to be american
        cause being african
        was inconvenient

        they say
        that in the multiverse

132

every version
of us
exists
so
wouldn't it be nice
if you could
find that version of you
who cared
so you could steal
his bio
for yourself
after all
it's still kinda you
right?

or
maybe we should
enshrine
the back stories
of wanna be
revolutionaries
in stone
to keep them
honest
so the stars
don't get
in their eyes

because
when the blind
try to lead
the blind
should know
whose got their
hand
in your pockets

Acknowledgments

My thanks to K. Nicole Wilson, Gil Duran, and Frank X Walker for their kind words and a willing to read the manuscript for this collection. Kenesha Williams for working on the cover for this special edition.

To my community of writers for their unfailing support, comradery, and inspiration.

To the Affrilachian Poets for your courage, your audacity, your raised voices, and your endless talent. The world is a better place with you in it.

To my mom and my brother for always being there and for your love, your belief, and your support.

And to the readers of my work who continue to remind me that what I do makes a difference in their lives.

About the Author

Gerald L. Coleman is a Philosopher, Theologian, Poet, and Scifi-Fantasy Author residing in Atlanta. Born in Lexington, he did his undergraduate work in Philosophy, English, and Religious Studies, followed by a Master's degree in Theology. His most recent poetry appears in, Pluck! The Journal of Affrilachian Arts & Culture, Drawn To Marvel: Poems From The Comic Books, Pine Mountain Sand & Gravel Vol. 18, Black Bone Anthology, the 10th Anniversary Issue of Diode Poetry Journal, and About Place Journal. His speculative fiction short stories appear in: The Science Fiction, Cyberfunk Anthology: *The City*, the *Rococoa* Anthology by Roaring Lion, the Urban Fantasy Anthology: *Terminus*, the 2019 JordanCon Anthology: *You Want Stories?*, *Dark Universe: Bright Empire*, and the upcoming Dystopian Anthology from Onyx Path Publishing. He is the author of the Epic Fantasy novel saga *The Three Gifts*, which currently includes *When Night Falls* (Book One) and *A Plague of Shadows* (Book Two). He has been a Guest Author at DragonCon, Boskone, Blacktasticon, JordanCon, Atlanta Science Fiction & Fantasy Expo, The Outer Dark Symposium, World Horror Con, Imaginarium, and Multiverse. He served as a Programme Content Consultant for WorldCon Dublin and the Director of the Fantasy Track for MultiverseCon.

He is a co-founder of the Affrilachian Poets and has released four collections of poetry entitled *the road is long, falling to earth, microphone check,* and *Nappy Metaphysic.* You can find him at Geraldcoleman.com.